THINK THEMES

For imaginative programme material
for outings and camps

by Frances Lane
with additional material by
Terry Watson

Cover design by Ron Branagan
Inside illustrations by Maarten Brom

1

© Printforce Limited

British Library Cataloguing in Publication Data
Lane, Frances
    Think themes : for imaginative programme material for outings and camps.
    1.   Activities for young persons
    I.   Title
    790.192

    ISBN 0-948834-41-2

CONTENTS

Page

13   London

21   "The Mikado"

27   Sailors

36   "The Wombles"

41   Hollywood

47   Pirates

51   The Wild West

56   Space

AN IDEAS WEB USING A SPACE THEME

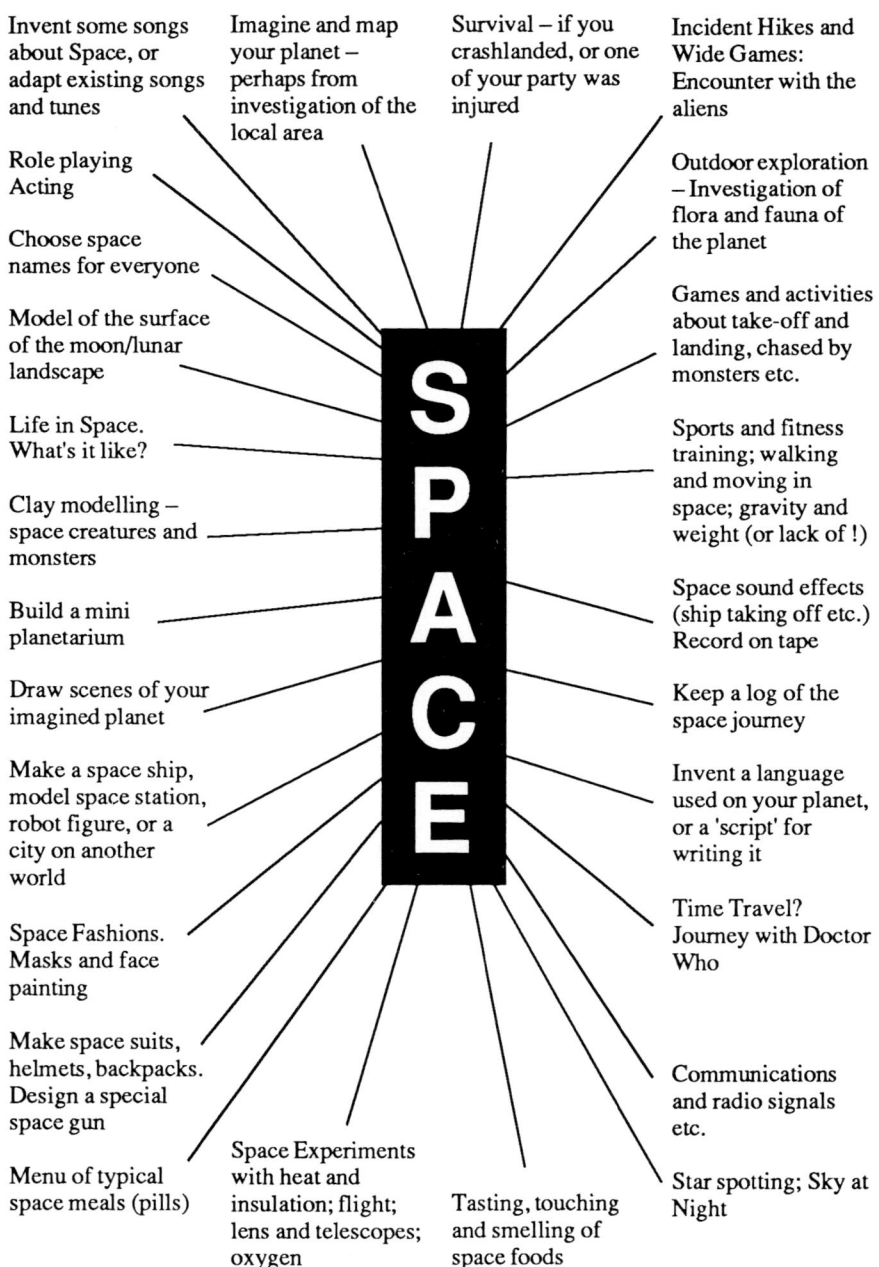

Invent some songs about Space, or adapt existing songs and tunes

Imagine and map your planet – perhaps from investigation of the local area

Survival – if you crashlanded, or one of your party was injured

Incident Hikes and Wide Games: Encounter with the aliens

Role playing Acting

Choose space names for everyone

Model of the surface of the moon/lunar landscape

Life in Space. What's it like?

Clay modelling – space creatures and monsters

Build a mini planetarium

Draw scenes of your imagined planet

Make a space ship, model space station, robot figure, or a city on another world

Space Fashions. Masks and face painting

Make space suits, helmets, backpacks. Design a special space gun

Menu of typical space meals (pills)

Space Experiments with heat and insulation; flight; lens and telescopes; oxygen

Tasting, touching and smelling of space foods

Outdoor exploration – Investigation of flora and fauna of the planet

Games and activities about take-off and landing, chased by monsters etc.

Sports and fitness training; walking and moving in space; gravity and weight (or lack of !)

Space sound effects (ship taking off etc.) Record on tape

Keep a log of the space journey

Invent a language used on your planet, or a 'script' for writing it

Time Travel? Journey with Doctor Who

Communications and radio signals etc.

Star spotting; Sky at Night

4

CAMP THEMES - Why bother?

A theme gives a sense of continuity to a camp, enabling various and varied activities to be gathered under one umbrella, tied together with a common link. Any activity can be included; all you need is even a vague connection between it and the chosen theme (or, do not even bother trying to find a link. Put in whatever activity you want, and set your members a competition by asking them what they think the link is, and adopt the most plausible explanation!).

This enables you to progress smoothly within a defined boundary - the fact that you define the boundary to suit yourself is neither here nor there! The members feel that everything they are doing is linked in with everything else. Even though the activities are widely different, they are connected within the theme, rather than being several disjointed activities which have no common link.

This also means that you can "recycle" activities and games, using them for more than one camp: just relabel them to fit the new theme, and present as new.

Anything can be used as a camp theme (to prove it, see "The Mikado", page 21!). There really are hundreds of things upon which to base a camp theme, besides the run-of-the-mill ones that come out time after time - and even they can be given a new lease of life.

Create a "Spiderweb" ideas-sheet: write the target word in the centre of a sheet of paper, and list things associated with it, and things associated with them, and so on. Then see how many of them can be worked into activities/games, or how they can be used to give old ideas new twists.

Almost before you know it, you will have the skeleton of a camp theme, especially if the "brain-storming" is done by more than one person - two or three people can "spark" each other off, keeping ideas coming. All you have to do then is to dress the ideas up a bit.

SAMPLE DAY'S PROGRAMME

(Elements of the programme and their timing can be adjusted to suit the ages and abilities of your members. This programme might suit children aged 10-14).

7.30	rise, breakfast, chores, notices, etc.
9.45	ACTIVITY PERIOD 1
11.00	"elevenses": drink and biscuits
11.15	ACTIVITY PERIOD 2
12.30	lunch
1.30	rest period: quiet activity: handicraft etc
2.00	ACTIVITY PERIOD 3
3.30	drink and biscuits
3.45	ACTIVITY PERIOD 4
5.30	dinner
6.30	rest period as before
7.00	ACTIVITY PERIOD 5 (Wide game?)
8.30	bed

There are five main activity periods each day: these can be broken into smaller segments, or two can be added together, wrapped around the "drink and biscuits" break for an extended activity - the exact timing depends upon the activities you are doing.

This gives a total activity time per day of 6 3/4 hours, including the two rest periods, during which sitting down activities can be done - camp logs, handicraft, etc., or giving members free time to read or play board games.

Note that activities also include "Free Time"!

Non-theme activities can be included pretty much as you wish - the theme should be a guide, not a straitjacket. A number of the themes given have activities run on bases - any activity could be done here, and points awarded according to the theme (i.e. "Pirates" - any activity completed would give the members more "treasure" to add to their "money bags": "Indians": add "scalps" to their lances, etc).

Not all of the given activities or games will be suitable to all ages and abilities: they can be scaled up/down to suit your particular members' needs/abilities.

Always plan a few more activities than you think you will need - just in case. The weather could turn, make a planned outdoor activity impractical, or an emergency could leave you a leader short. It helps to have a few planned indoor activities/games in hand which can be run by the minimum of leaders, in case of need.

Recurring Items

There are a number of activities that crop up in several themes listed in this book: to save repetition, they are detailed here, and only mentioned in the text.

1.   Shelters

If the campsite has sufficient natural resources, each team builds its own shelter (caution members to have respect for growing things, and not to pull them about more than they have to). Fallen branches can be assembled into a basic shape and "thatched" with ferns or long grass, taking advantage of natural formations.

If the site does not have the facility, shelters can be made with bamboo garden canes, and fastened with elastic-band-lashing or proper lashings (an introduction to knots and lashings, as well as simple pioneering). "Thatching" can be done with OLD bedsheets or blankets, or pieces of plastic sheeting.

If shelters are on the programme, let them be done towards the beginning of the camp, so that the teams have a little hidey-hole where they can meet up. Also, it may take days to add the "finishing touches"!

Once built, shelters can be weather-tested by a leader with a bucket of water, while the team goes inside it with their swimwear on. The resulting deluge teaches members indelibly the need for stout construction! (Note: pour the water on slowly rather than tossing it, unless the purpose is to demolish the shelter completely!)

2.   Fires

If woodfires are allowed on the campsite the members can learn to lay and light their own fires (perhaps with the traditional "two matches"!). Once lit, they can cook something simple - sausage, piece of toast, etc. There are many kinds of fire, but the pyramid fire is the one generally used. Teach members fire-prevention/precautions as well.

3.   Tracking/Stalking

Illustrations of basic tracking signs are readily available in a number of publications. Start with large, clear signs, and gradually make them less easy to spot, smaller and blending in more with the background. Or use coloured wool trails - start off with bright colours, and gradually move to greens and browns, to make the members look harder.

Stalking can be introduced in games in which the members have to creep up on a leader without being seen or heard, or have to go from A to B without being spotted.

4.   Models

Quite a few themes deal with dressing-up. If there are not the resources for the members to costume themselves, they could make a costume for a model: "Barbie" dolls (or "Action Man" for boys who would not be seen playing with dolls!). The dolls can be dressed with material scraps; fitting could be done with a couple of stiches here and there, or with a suitable glue.

Failing that, the models can be stand-up card figures, in which case the costumes would be cut out of paper, with fold over tabs to keep them on the figures. Or you can give the members figures drawn on paper, to be costumed with coloured pens or coloured sticky paper.

5.   Diorama

Once the models are made, each team makes a backing sheet to display the models, filling in the details according to the theme of the costumes.

6.   Murals

All members each draw/colour one sheet of paper on a specific theme: when done, all the panels are put together and displayed. This, and the previous activity, only really work if you have walls to hang the pictures from - unless you wish to hang a mural in a tent?

7.   Signalling

Semaphore: pipe-cleaner figures (or stand-up card figures) can be made with movable arms, so that members can play sending messages to each other. Morse: can be sent a dozen different ways: light, whistle, flag, smoke-signals, etc. One and two character letters are: A E I M N T. Add O S H (all easy to remember characters) and words can be sent. Three character letters: D G K O R S U W. All other letters have four characters.

8.   Matchbox boats

For sites with a stream. Use the tray from a standard sized matchbox (not the wooden ones). Cut off one end panel. Then cut between the bottom and sides until the loose ends can meet. Sellotape together. Cut off the excess bottom until it fits the shape of the bows of the boat; Sellotape the seams thoroughly. Fix a cocktail/barbecue stick mast with a dab of Plasticene/Blue Tak. Cut a square of paper and thread onto the mast for a sail. (Stick the top of the sail to the mast, or it will uncurl over the top of the mast). Place it on a stretch of calm water and let it go. Perhaps the members can put a contact address on the sail, asking anyone who finds it to write and say where it was found: see whose went furthest down-stream. (A boat as described above floated for more than eight hours when tested in a bowl of water: if you want yours to last that long, make sure all edges and corners are well sealed!).

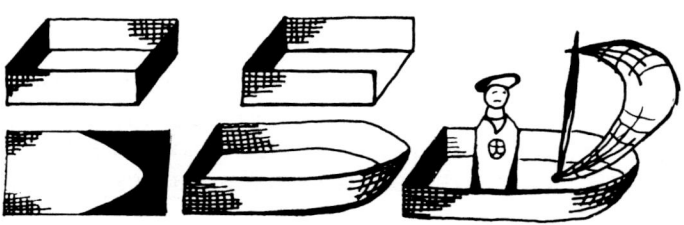

If you use a "household" sized matchbox, you could make a two-masted ship, perhaps with a full set of sails. Types of boat can vary with the theme: the basic pattern remains the same, but the type of sail varies: Vikings would have a large sail, the top corners secured with cotton/cord to the stern, feluccas would have lateen sails (which involves fitting a yard). Perhaps older members could rig their boat properly, with boom and rigging, and see which can sail nearest the wind.

10

9. Prayer boats

Made as above. Instead of a mast, fix a 1"-2" length of taper. As evening/night draws in, take the members to the stream, to a place where they can see it for some distance in both directions. Leaders take the boats upstream, light the tapers and set them adrift, so that the members can see the fleet of lights drifting past. As the boats approach the members' position, a leader with them reads a prayer and asks the members to pray quietly to themselves for as long as they can see the lights. This can be a very effective way of ending a day, given the right weather conditions.

Household sized matchboxes can have a sail of coloured Cellophane in front of the tapers, so that the members see multi-coloured lights.

GAMES

Many types of 'wide game' can be used by giving them different titles and "plots" - some of the more common types are:

Variation 1

Cards are spread around the playing area, or leaders are given a set of cards each. Members must a) bring back all of one design/colour; b) bring back a set of one of each design/colour; c) bring back any card they find, regardless of design/colour. Any of these variations can alternatively be played with strands of coloured wool.

Whichever variation you use, members must bring one card back to base before they can go looking for the next.

Variation 2

Two teams, either members vs leaders or two teams of members. Team A have to get from one place to another without being tagged by Team B. Those tagged lose a life - a strand of wool, tied loosely about the upper arm (NOT nylon wool; it will not break if pulled; it may burn fingers). Members tagged must return to their base for another life. Members tagged must take the captured life back to their base before they can capture anybody else. The team with most lives at the end of time wins.

Depending on the plot, Team A may be carrying items which Team B must capture as before.

Variation 3

Tracking/stalking games. Members have to stay uncaught by the opposition as long as possible. Those caught are out. They may have to reach a certain place to get home. This is a variation often played after dark.

LONDON

Leaders' Names: London Statues: Boadicea, Nelson, Peter Pan, Eros, Queen Victoria, etc.

Teams: a)   Underground lines: District, Jubilee, Circle, Piccadilly, Bakerloo, etc.

or

b)   Bridges: Tower, London, Vauxhall, Albert, Chelsea, Blackfriars, etc.

Places:

Campsite
Leader's tent
Other leaders' tents

Members' tents
Washrooms
Local shop(s)
Dining area
First aid area

City of London
10 Downing Street
Houses of
  Parliament
Old Bailey
Petticoat Lane
Stock Exchange
Cafe Royal
Barts Hospital

ACTIVITIES

1.   Models. Each member makes a costume of a London character: Beefeaters, Yeomen Warders, Chelsea Pensioners, Guardsmen, Pearly Kings/Queens.

2.   Diorama. To back up their models: Buckingham Palace for Guards, the Tower for Warders, street market for Pearlies, etc.

3.   Crown Jewels. Either cut out and stick predrawn patterns, or members make their own, realism depending upon age and ability.

4.   Pearlies. Members costume themselves as Pearly Kings/Queens with small white round stickers in pat-

terns which they design for themselves.

5. Music Hall. Each team (and leaders!) provide a "turn" for a Music Hall entertainment, with traditional Cockney songs. Following on from the above, try traditional Cockney food: jellied eels, pie and mash.

6. Lord Mayor's Show. Members design and make mini floats for the Lord Mayor's Show. Any themes you/they wish, either in teams or individually.

7. Building Bridges. Provide each team with materials to build a model of one of London's bridges (perhaps their "team bridge", if teams are named after bridges). Models can range from predrawn cut out and stick patterns, junk sculpture, mini pioneering (cocktail/barbecue sticks, bamboo canes) or the real thing, over a stream if the campsite has one.

8. Tower Bridge. In any one of the above variations; see which team can build the most realistic (working!) model.

9. Boat Race. Matchbox boats, or static paper/card/model displays.

10. Cutty Sark. Pioneer raft-building, either models or full sized, used on a local pond/stream. Hold "Clipper-ship" races - water stunts and games.

11. Rhyming Slang. Libraries have books of both Cockney and other rhyming slang. Or the members could invent their own rhyming slang terms.

12. Pudding Lane. The fire started in a baker's shop. Members try cooking/baking, either on fires or with "proper" ovens.

13. Monument. Teams build a camp gate/noticeboard/flagpole, to whatever design they wish.

14. "Parliamentary Debate". Pick a subject that will get your members going, and have a properly organised debate, with speakers for and against, and a vote afterwards. Either a leader or a member acts as "Mr. Speaker", to keep order.

15. Old Bailey. A leader has been "arrested" for committing a crime (breaking a camp rule??) and is put on trial. Select judge, prosecuting and defending counsel, and witnesses for and against. The rest of the members make up the jury. Leaders could act as advisers to Counsel as well as being called as witnesses. If the jury return a "guilty" verdict, then the judge passes sentence: perhaps give minutes in the "stocks" while the members have free rein with a stack of wet sponges, or anything else that the members will enjoy.

16. Fleet Street. Each team produces a camp newspaper, or all members co-produce a joint camp newspaper, with all members encouraged to contribute even a little item - drawing, article, etc. The results can be displayed and circulated.

17. St. Paul's. Each team takes responsibility for the morning/evening prayer for one day each, as well as choosing the grace for each day's meals. (If the members write their own prayers/graces, save them for later use at regular meetings as well). On one day at camp, have an act of worship; each team produces one part of it, and is responsible for organising and running it. Give them a theme to work to if necessary.

18. Trooping the Colour. The annual ceremony came about because of the habit of Trooping (showing) the Regimental Colour to the troops, so that they could recognise it in battle, and would know where to regroup. This leads into the Union Flag, your own organisation flag if it has one, and local flags and coats or arms, going into the history behind them. Ask your members

BEEFEATER

SWEEP

THE GREAT FIRE

to design their own flag for the camp, which has to take into account the "history" and location of the camp.

19. <u>London Invaders</u>. Normans, Romans, Vikings and Danes all conquered London (as well as Boadicea, who sacked it). London's history leads into local history of the area where you normally meet, or of the campsite area - local museums/churches, especially Norman/Saxon.

20. <u>London Walls</u>. On bases, with each base named after one of the London gates (Aldgate, Newgate, etc). As each team/member does the required activity (which could be anything), they mark in that gate on their maps and go on to the next gate.

21. <u>Fire of London</u>. Firelighting OR Safety at Camp - what to do in the event of a fire, etc.

22. <u>Lord Mayor's Banquet</u>. A special meal, with all members dressed up, perhaps inviting the Lord Mayor (Camp Warden or special visitor).

GAMES

1. <u>The Ceremony of the Keys</u>. Each night at the Tower, the Warders ceremoniously do the rounds, locking up the Tower and handing over the keys to the night guards. Play as Variation 1 or use real keys in a smaller area: give each team a magnet and see how many they can locate in a relay system.

2. <u>Chimney Sweeps</u>. In the last century, children of a young age were "employed" to help sweep chimneys. Set up an obstacle course to represent the inside of a chimney - with narrow tunnels, awkward bends, ropes to climb etc. Winner is the one who pops their head out of the chimmney top in the fastest time.

3. The Romans are Coming! Play as Variation 2, with the Londoners trying to escape from the Roman invaders.

4. Speakers' Corner. Each member must speak for one minute on any (given?) subject without hesitation or repetition, despite possible hecklers.

5. Gunpowder Plot. Can be played as Variation 1 or 2, with pictures of fireworks, or two teams, the Yeomen trying to capture the Plotters. (Perhaps wind up with a small safe firework display!).

6. I'm all right, Jack. Variation 1. The sets of cards carry the three national flags that make up the Union Flag (and the Welsh Flag, too). Teams must go out together to find a set of cards, one of each flag, only going back to base when they have the set. They exchange the flags for a Union Flag and go out to find another set. They may challenge any other teams they see, to try to rob them of any flags they have got. Each team shows how many Union Flags it has; whichever team has the most can take the other team's flags, as long as the capturing team does not have that flag already. If both teams have the same number of Union Flags, they tie: neither can take any of the other's. So any team who wants to challenge must gamble that the other team has fewer Union Flags. A team with only a few Union Flags must make sure that it stays out of the way!.

7. Sports. London Marathon - Test Match (the Oval) - Cup Final (Wembley) - Wimbledon: all provide ideas for silly sports/games.

8. Captain Blood. He tried to steal the Crown Jewels, and nearly got away with it. Play as Variation 1, with the cards carrying the name/picture of pieces of the Regalia. Or play Variation 2, with the one side trying to capture Captain Blood's men to confiscate the Jewels they are carrying.

9. Walls of London. Two teams, Londoners and Invaders (whichever). Londoners have to build a wall to keep the Invaders out (with blocks, line of squeezy bottles, etc.). The Invaders roll soft balls at the wall (distance depending on age and ability) to knock the wall down. See how much is still standing at the end of time. Invaders will need a good supply of soft balls. Then twop teams.

10. Thames Barges. Various items hidden around the playing area. Each team gets into its boat (a loop of rope which they get inside and hold up round them) and sail around, seeing how much cargo they can pick up and a) bring each item back to the Port of London (base) one at a time, or b) keep going until they cannot carry any more!

11. Boat Race. Each team has a row of chairs at one end of the playing area, facing the start. The ones nearest the start have batons. They take their chairs to the end of the line and hand the baton down. The new end member "rows" up to the far end of the line as soon as the baton is handed down. See which team can row the fastest until all members are over the finish line.

12. Trooping the Colour. Variation 1, with coloured card/wool strands.

13. Tower of London. Variation 1, with the cards making up a picture of the Tower.

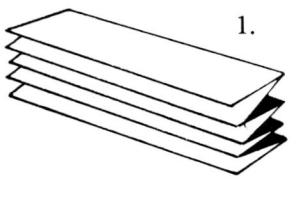

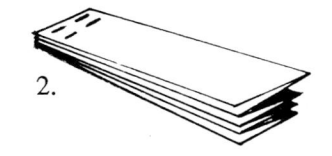

JAPANESE FAN

1. Pleat a sheet of paper each pleat 1" wide

2. Staple one end of fan

3. Cut shapes out of both edges

4. Unfold fan

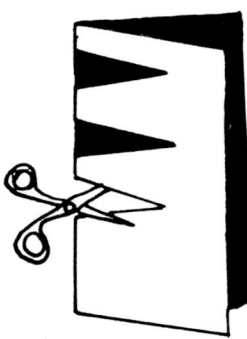

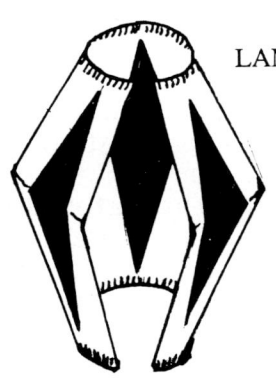

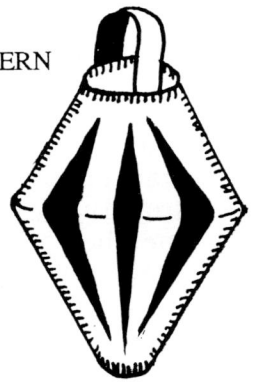

LANTERN

1. Fold sheet of paper in half. Make equal cuts from folded edge, about half way across

2. Open out and glue the two ends together

3. Glue on a small strip of paper for handle

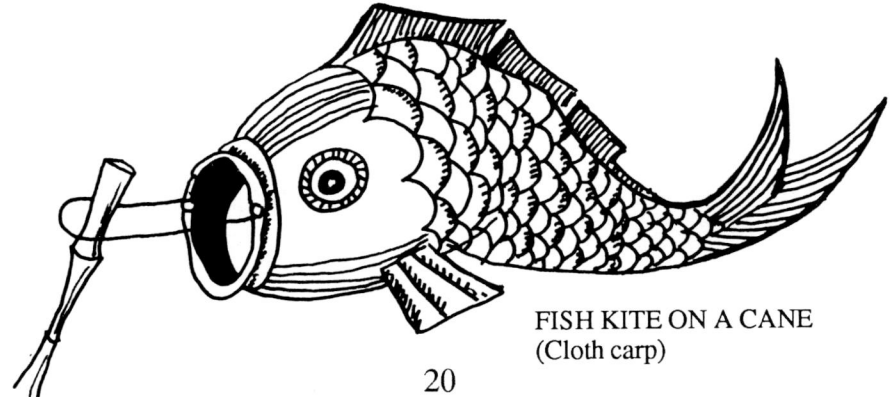

FISH KITE ON A CANE
(Cloth carp)

20

"THE MIKADO"

Leaders: The Mikado (Camp Warden or special visitor)
             Ko-Ko [Lord High Executioner] (Camp leader)
             Poo-Bah [Lord High Everything Else] (Assistant
             camp leader)
             Nanki-Poo, Katisha, Yum-Yum, Pitti-Sing, Pish-
             Tush, Go-To, Peeb-Bo

Teams: Citizens, Guards, Nobles, Coolies

Places: Camp area   The Town of Titipu
             Leaders' tents   Knightsbridge
             Members' tents   Town Square
             Dining area   Cha ha (teahouse)

ACTIVITIES

1.   Cha no yu. A small, family-sized teahouse. Construst
     shelters to represent this.

2.   Models. Costumes for Samurai/Geisha girls. Japanese
     girls have a set of dolls which they bring out for the
     girls' festival. Boys have a festival of their own when
     cloth carp fly from poles outside their houses.

3.   Diorama. Each team makes the background and
     arranges its models: other teams try to guess the story
     behind each diorama, working on the background, the
     placing and pose of the models.

4.   Origami. There are many books available from
     libraries, giving traditional patterns and others which
     may be easier for less-nimble fingers.

5.   Papercraft. Making Coolie hats, folding paper fans,
     Japanese lanterns, paper flowers to decorate dining
     area.

6.   Kites. These are of many types, from traditional box-

kites to newspaper/plastic bag types. Older members could try to construct load-carrying kites.

7. <u>Miniature Gardens</u>. Both the cha ya and the cha no yu often had formal gardens, elaborately laid out in traditional patterns to help people to relax. Give each member a small container to make their own Japanese gardens with twigs, pebbles, etc. Teams could be given larger tubs or trays to make a team garden. See who can create the most authentic Japanese look.

8. <u>Windchimes</u>. Cut bamboo canes into small pieces, between 1" and 3" long, of different thicknesses to make different sounds. These are to be strung on a small disc of thin wood/thick card, with holes around the edge from which to hang the pieces, and a hole in the centre to take a hanging loop. Make sure that all pieces are hung about the same height, to strike each other properly.

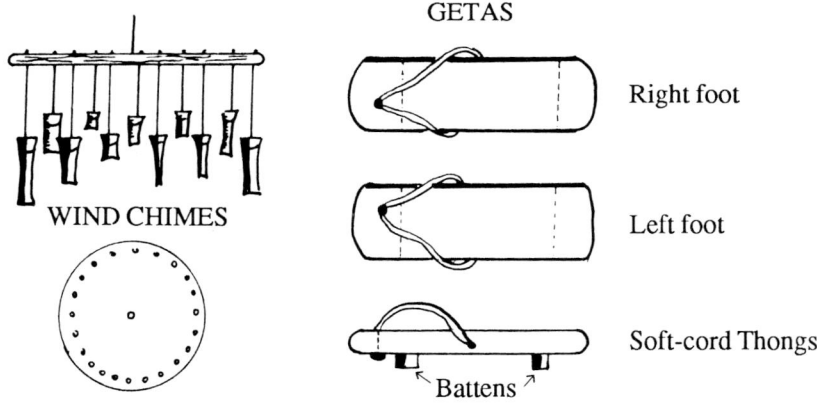

WIND CHIMES

GETAS

Right foot

Left foot

Soft-cord Thongs

Battens

9. <u>Getas</u>. Traditional Japanese sandals, rather like wooden flip-flops. A foot sized piece of wood (with edges and corners rounded off) has two wooden battens fixed underneath, in about the positions shown. The front batten comes under the ball of the foot, the back one about half way in from the heel, where the maximum pressure comes. A hole, drilled about 1/3 of the

way in from the big toe side, takes a doubled cord; the middle is pushed through and knotted, and the two ends are taken back to each side and secured on the side. Leave them slack enough for the member's foot. The cord goes between big and second toes.

10. Chopsticks. Thin dowelling rods, cut into 9-10" lengths, with the cut ends smoothed to avoid splinters. Real chopsticks have rounded eating ends and square hand held ends, which are often decorated. Younger members could merely decorate their hand held ends; older members could square theirs off before decorating. The eating ends are NOT decorated. Then let members use them at their next meal (as long as it does not include gravy!).

11. Knots/lashings. This links in via Japanese lashing, which is a method of square lashing, used in pioneering. This leads into pioneering projects, with bamboo canes (which also fit the theme) or full sized spars.

12. Fishing Boats. Matchbox boats.

13. Prayer Boats. The Japanese use a form of this on their Hiroshima/Nagasaki Remembrance Day. Perhaps a prayer for peace would not be amiss.

14. The "Willow Pattern". The familiar blue willow pattern crockery is based on a Japanese legend of two lovers who are kept apart by a broken bridge. Tell the members the story: show them a piece of plate, or a picture of one, if you can, and let them act out the story, with pictures, plays, puppets, etc.

15. Thinking. The main Japanese religion is Shinto. Your library will have books on the basics: discuss with your members, and talk about different religions/ways of life; encourage them to think about their own spiritual commitment, and how they can grow close to God in their own way. Discuss the many different ways that

23

people worship: encourage members to tolerate other beliefs/ways of life that they themselves do not share.

16. Flower Arranging. Let eqach member collect and arrange grasses, ferns, etc., perhaps for table centres. Chrysanthemums, etc. for flower making (coloured tissue paper/paper "hanky" tissue).

17. "The Mikado". Tell the story of the opera, and let the members illustrate scenes from it with plays, mimes, drawings, etc. Perhaps a video or audio tape can be played for them.

18. Food. Rice, sweet potatoes, beans, fish. O-mochi - special rice dish. Sashimi - sliced raw fish. Sukiyaki - mixture of beef, onions, beans, mushrooms, bamboo shoots and other vegetables. The members might like to try traditional Japanese recipes - eaten with chopsticks, of course. Libraries have "international" cook books.

19. Brush writing. Traditionally done with short bristled stiff brushes, but ordinary paint brushes will do - make the paint a bit thicker than uusal, to help reduce the chances of it running. Members could make decorative scrolls, either by painting pre-drawn patterns, or inventing their own, with authentic (or authentic looking) Japanese characters.

20. Invite your "Mikado" to a special meal one evening. Decorate the dining area with the lanterns, windchimes, and flowers that the members have made. Everybody wears "kimonos" (dressing gowns) with the coolie hats and getas, and eats Japanese food with chopsticks, seated on cushions on the floor. Tatami - straw mats and Futon - roll out beds (sleeping bags).

21. Pen Pals. Follow on from camp. Find out if your members would be interested in obtaining (and keeping!) Japanese pen pals of a similar age, and encourage

members to lean about Japanese customs/language, daily life and so on.

22. Japanese Art/Ink Painting - or colour drawings of topical/typical scenes, or blow painting with straws. Portraits, landscapes (waterfalls, mountains, forests), plants, birds and animals.

23. Build a Model Pagoda (odds and ends), or a Torii (ceremonial archway) at the entrance to your camp site.

GAMES

1. Nanki-Poo has run away from Katisha, and all the Townspeople have to search for him. Any Variation 1.

2. Messengers. The Mikado has sent Messengers to Titipu, whom the teams must guard on their journey. Each Messenger (leader) has one team to guard it, but teams must try to rob other teams' Messengers. Leaders have strands of wool, different colours per team. They set off, then each team has to a) rob other Messengers of a strand of wool at a time, and b) prevent their own Messenger from being robbed. They rob other Messengers by tagging them; he gives them a strand of wool which they take to their own Messenger (meaning that they have got to find him first!). They may rob any other team they see with their own colour wool, and take that back to their Messenger, too. The team whose Messenger has the most own colour strands at the end of time wins.

3. Shopping List. The Mikado is coming to Titipu, and the Townspeople have to prepare a feast for him, by fetching cards with different foods written on them. Can be played as Variation 1, or with the cards spread around a smaller area, and teams going in relay to fetch specified cards - first team to finish. Or it can be run on activity bases, with each person/team getting items on their shopping list ticked off as they complete activities.

4. Chopstraws. Played like the old game "Jackstraws", but with chopstick sized pieces. A handful of cocktail/barbecue sticks is held just above the floor, and allowed to drop down, falling anywhere. Members must pick them up, one at a time, without moving any of the other sticks. If that happens, the next person takes a turn, and so on. Can be played either inter-team with a super final for the winner from each team) or all in.

5. Chopstick relay. Each team has one pair of chopsticks and a small dish of dried peas or similar. They must pick up a pea in the chopsticks and carry it to a saucer some distance away. Dropped peas are picked up where they fell. The first team to finish, or the team that picks up most in the time is the winner. To get a bit sillier, give older members long garden canes, and tell them to chopstick carry an object a set distance.

6. Wrestling. Judo or Sumo style (well supervised, of course).

7. Playing Cards. Knockout competition - play any card game in teams, ending up with one winning team. A favourite Japanese card game is Hyakunin Isshu (played only at New Year).

SAILORS

Leaders: Christopher Columbus, Vasco da Gama, Ferdinand Magellan, Sir Walter Raleigh, Clare Francis, Sir Francis Chichester, Captain Cook, Admiral Nelson, Sir Francis Drake, Noah!

Teams: Golden Hind, Victory, Beagle, Endeavour, Discovery, Bounty, Ark Royal, Gipsy Moth (subdivide into Port and Starboard Watches, if desired).

Places:

Leaders' tents	Quarterdeck
Members' tents	Fo'c'sle
Kitchen area	Galley
Dining area	Gundeck
Flagpole	Mainmast
First aid area	Cockpit

ACTIVITIES

1. Models of sailors' uniforms, past and present, of different nationalities.

2. Boats. Card cut out boats of different types: galleons, square-riggers, galleys.

3. The Ark. Get the exact description from Genesis: each team build an Ark going only on that description. If made from card, see whose floats the best in "rough seas", as the original Ark would have had to do!

4. Diorama. Any of the above can be backed by suitable team dioramae.

5. Weather. Basic meteorology. The camp could run a small weather station, with teams responsible for one of the (home made?) instruments, keeping a daily log of the weather conditions.

6. Pioneering. Teams make a raft, canoe, or coracle, in any kind of model format (card, cocktail/barbecue stick, etc) or for real, for them to try on any local safe water.

7. Dugout canoe. Each member makes a dugout canoe out of a small round piece of wood, perhaps 3" diameter by about 1' long. It can have outriggers if desired. Then have a flotation test to see whose is most stable.

8. Watchkeeping. Use "ship time" for the camp, with the bells properly struck to change watches or to announce meals, start of next activity, etc. "Real" watchkeeping can be introduced more or less accurately, depending upon members' ages.

9. Hornpipe. With the aid of a tape of "the" Hornpipe, teams invent their own hornpipe, to be performed at the campfire/entertainment. The original hornpipe mimed sailors' activities - hauling on ropes, etc: perhaps the members' dances can mime camp activities?

10. Sea Shanties. There are many books of old folk songs and traditional sea shanties available. One kind of shanty was used when heaving on ropes, weighing the anchor, and so on: everybody heaved on the chorus, and rested on the verse, ensuring that everybody pulled together. The members could experiment to see if this method is more effective than everybody just pulling anyhow. Members could be taught shanties to sing at the campfire. This also provides a handicraft item, with teams/members illustrating a shanty with mime, drawings, etc.

11. Sea Stories. There are many real life sea stories, from RNLI rescues to naval heroes such as Jack Cornwell VC. The chosen story/ies can be illustrated in a following handicraft session.

12. Bo'suns's Call. Introduce older members to the bo'suns's call, and teach them how to pipe. Once learned, the calls can be used to announce meals, etc.

13. Signalling. The International system of flag signalling is available from many sources. Single flags spell out messages, or combinations of two or three flags can stand for special messages. If you have access to a set of flags (and a flagpole!) you could use them to send "long distance" messages to your members. Morse and Semaphore can also be taught and used long distance.

14. Swimming/water safety/lifesaving.

15. Knots. Start with simple "plain" knots, many of which are derived from sailing days (reef knot, sheet bend, anchor hitch, jury mast knot, etc.) and work up to sailors' fancy knots.

16. Navigation. Map and compass. Navigating by the stars.

17. Swinging the Lead. The term for someone getting away with doing less work than other people comes from sailing days. When a ship was getting close to land, a sailor had to throw a long line, weighted at the end, with the rope marked in different ways every so often. From this he could tell how deep the water was. This was tiring work, but not nearly so hard as climbing up and down the masts and rigging! If there is any safe water on the campsite, teams could chart the depth at various points (from a raft, if they have one), using a sounding rod marked in feet, seeing how far up the rod the water comes when the end is on the bottom.

18. Fathoms. The reason that the naval measure of a fathom equals six feet is very simple - that is about the armspan of a lot of men - every man was his own ruler! The members can work out their own armspans - how long would their "fathoms" be? From there they can go on to other personal measurements -length of forearm,

29

length of stride, of foot, and so on, noting down their own "ruler marks". Then they can try measuring rope, or pacing out a distance, seeing who gets closest to the true answer.

19. Charting/mapmaking. Each team has a blank map of the campsite, with only a couple of features to help them to orient it. They then map the rest of the area, and draw a scale map. See who gets the closest.

20. Handicraft. Members make sailors' round hats or cocked-hats (with a front-piece and a band to hold it on; older members could try to make a "proper" one) and card cutlasses.

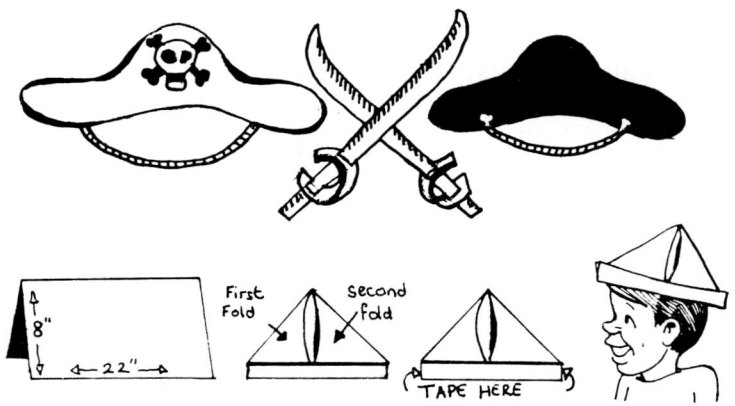

21. Gale Warning. There are 28 weather areas around Britain used for shipping forecasts. A map of these can be had from various sources. A game can be made by giving the teams a blank map of the UK and a list of areas; see if they can match them up.

22. R.N.L.I. Tell the members about the R.N.L.I., and the sort of things that lifeboatmen do as routine duty. They could illustrate an incident, and might be interested in "adopting" the R.N.L.I. as the group charity.

23. <u>Sailing/canoeing</u>.

24. <u>"Land Sailing"</u>. Provide each team with some large cardboard boxes, and a stack of odds and ends. They build their own ship on land, by putting the cartons end to end to make the body of the ship, and decorating with mast, sail, anchor, etc. (a "mast" can be easily obtained by putting the boxes to either side of a convenient sapling!). The ships can be of any type; Viking, man-'o-war, etc.

25. <u>Logbooks</u>. Sailors keep detailed logbooks, recording everything that happens on a voyage. Each member/team could keep a log, with drawings, adding to it every day (rest period activity), or they could all produce one Camp Log, which can be decorated, and have photos added after the camp, to provide a display item on future occasions.

26. <u>Press Gang</u>. Camp newspaper, either team or all in.

27. <u>Homework</u>. After the camp, challenge members to find out about their team name/ leaders' camp names. Why are those ships and people famous?

GAMES

1. <u>Naval Gunrun</u>. Players have to convey across an obstacle course, a trek cart, soap box cart, or shopping trolley without the bag, with added "equipment" to be transported through the course. Or the teams could play Variation 1, with the collected cards making up a picture of a naval gun and limber.

2. <u>Ship on the Rocks</u>. This has many names - "Port and Starboard", "Captain's Coming Aboard", etc.

3. <u>Setting Sails</u>. Each team has a model/picture of a sailing boat. Play as Variation 1: the cards have the names of sails on them, and the teams have to put their cards in the right places on their ship. First team to set all sails wins.

4. <u>Cat o' nine tails</u>. Either play as a "pin the tail on the donkey", except that each team's cat has to have nine tails, or as a wide game, with the tails hidden around the playing area. It could be played with only <u>eight</u> tails per cat, and one over, so that only one team can get all nine tails. It could be made into a "base raiding" game, with teams pinching each other's tails - the team who ends up with nine (or the most) tails wins.

5. <u>Splice the Mainbrace</u>. Each team is given lengths of rope, one per person. They have to be joined together to make one continuous length. This can be done <u>en masse</u>, or as a relay (either as all number 1s going together, then all No 2s, etc., or that each team's No. 2 goes as soon as the No 1 returns).

6. <u>Navel Action</u> (not a mis-spelling!). Each team is given a loop of rope, big enough for them all to stand inside. They hold it up around their stomachs and carry out the next activity like that - you can make the next activity an obstacle course, or a cruise through the woods. Each team must stay inside its own "ship". This could be

made into a raiding game, where each ship tries to capture other ships' flags.

7.   Raising the Anchor. Pioneering. Each team constructs a derrick to lift a set weight a set distance. Construction must include a way of tying-off the rope, so that the members do not have to keep handing on. (A good time to test the effectiveness of sea shanties!).

8.   Running out the Guns. Pioneering. Each team constructs a block and tackle to move a set weight a set distance, horizontally or vertically. If horizontally, then the object must be moved away from the team, as a naval cannon was run up for firing. Try different tackles, and see the advantages/disadvantages of each.

9.   Raising the Mast. Pioneering. Teams construct a "giraffe" to hoist a spar vertically: the design must include a way of tying-off the raised spar safely.

10.   Camels at Sea. "Camels" were a method used to lessen a ship's draught. Two barges/lighters were loaded with sand or water, then lashed to either side of the boat. The sand or water was pumped out; this made the barges rise in the water, and, as the boat was lashed to them, it was raised, too. If you can get access to three small boats (rowing boats, canoes - NOT kayaks!) the members could try making camels; can they lift the central boat right out of the water? Will their lashings stand up to the strain they will be subject to? Care must be taken to empty both camels evenly, or else the strain becomes much greater.

11. Rowing Race. Each team has a plank, narrow enough for them to straddle, long enough for them all to get on it. The end one is the Cox'n, and faces the others, steering them round/through/over obstacles. They can either hold the plank up and walk backwards (but be careful if some members are much shorter than others in their team!) or they can sit on it, and "row" by digging their heels in and pushing. The cox'n must give the time for the strokes, or the "oars" might get tangled!

12. Lightships. A dark game. The leaders are lightships, each with a torch. The members are ships who have to navigate past the rocks (marked by the lightships) and reach harbour safely. Any member caught in torchlight has run aground, and is sunk.

13. Spithead Review. Each team makes bunting out of crepe paper/odds and ends and decorates its tent and a section of camp, perhaps running bunting between trees.

14. Grog Ration. Variation 1. Members go out and collect cards to get their grog. They may either return each card to base, or keep going after more - BUT leaders may tag them, in which case they lose all the grog they have got on them at the time. So they can choose to play safe, or hope that they can run faster than leaders!

15. Man the Rigging. Tree climbing, perhaps with (home made) rope ladders and suspended ropes to climb up/down/across. Protect trees from abrasions from ropes.

16. Battleships. Can be played as normal, on paper, but as team vs team, or if the teams are large enough, use members as the pieces, drawing chalk lines on the floor, with the "ships" moving as the caller decides.

17. Convoys. Optional dark game. Each team is a convoy of merchant ships trying to get through to harbour. Leaders (or another team) are the sumbarines. Ships caught are sunk, their cargoes captured: the whole convoy has to return to the starting harbour to take on new cargo. The team should be in "convoy pattern" - spread out a little, but in sight/contact. If you like, you can invent a way for the ships to throw depth-charges at the sumbarines!

18. Gun Drill. Played like "Zoos", but each rank is called for one of the men who formed a gun team - Chief Gunner, Gunlayer, Rammer, and so on. Each runs when their name is called: on "Run guns out" the whole team runs.

19. All aboard the Skylark. Silly stunts/races.

20. Invite "First Sea Lord" (Camp warden/special visitor) to dinner aboard ship. Name the menu after sailors' food; "dress ship" with bunting, etc.

THE WOMBLES

Leaders: Great Uncle Bulgaria (camp leader), Tobermorey (QM), Madame Cholet (Chief Cook), Miss Adelaide (First-aider), Alderney (Assistant Cook), Bungo, Wellington, Tomsk, Orinoco, MacWomble, Cousin Yellowstone

Teams: Let each member/team pick its name from an atlas, like real Wombles.

ACTIVITIES

1. Womble Stories. There are four Wombles books, by Elisabeth Beresford: The Wombles, The Wandering Wombles, The Wombles at Work and Wombling Free. One chapter could be read each day, and the members can illustrate it with mimes, plays, or pictures.

2. Anti-Litter Campaign. Wombles are VERY anti-litter. Members can design posters for the campsite/normal meeting place/schools/libraries, highlighting the problems that litter causes, and what can be done about it. Discuss with members how they, as young people, could help to solve the problem, and what they think adults should do about it.

3. Matchbox Scavenge Hunt. Each member has a standard-sized matchbox, and the one who can get the most objects into it, natural as well as litter, wins. Points for variety as well as quantity.

4. Womble Spelling. Give each member a sheet of paper with the words "THE WOMBLES" written down one side. They have to spot natural objects which begin with each letter, and write it down opposite its letter. See who can spell the words first. Two different objects are needed for the "e"s. A leader may be necessary to help members with writing.

5. <u>Wombling Free</u>. Each members is given a Womble bag (plastic carrier) and goes out to collect litter; the one who collects the biggest variety wins. OR, "seed" the area with "clean" litter - odds and ends, egg boxes etc. The members collect as before, but now they must make something out of what they collect, just like real Wombles. Make sure that all the uncollected odds and ends are picked up at the end of the session!

6. <u>Pollution Hunt</u>. Each team goes with a leader on a walk around the campsite or local area. Ask them to look out for things which are spoiling the area, whether dumped rubbish, dirty streams, heavily used roads, etc. When all the teams get back, get them to compare lists: lead into a discussion of what they think could be done.

7. <u>Make a Womble</u>. Members make Wombles, by either (or both) of the following methods: a) make two wool pom-poms, one larger than the other. Tie them snugly together to make the head and body of a Womble. Then decorate; add features, arms and legs. B) Cut two fat figure eight shapes from material, making one loop of the eight bigger than the other. Put them together, right sides in, and sew together, leaving a gap in the bottom of the bigger loop. Turn the material right side out through the gap, stuff with cut up stockings/foam chips, and sew closed. Decorate as above.

8. <u>Junk Sculpture</u>. Each member/team makes a model out of odds and ends, of your or their choice.

9. <u>Collages</u>. Each member/team collects natural objects and makes a picture/model from them, theme to be your/their choice.

10. <u>Natural Painting</u>. Members collect natural objects as above, but use them to paint a picture by extracting their natural juices. Different grasses, twisted and crushed, give different shades of green: then there are berries, leaves, and different kinds of soil.

    <u>Important</u>: Make sure members wash their hands thoroughly after this activity, and that they do NOT eat any berries, etc., that they find without checking first with a leader: to be on the safe side, say "No" to anything they find.

11. <u>Womble of the Week</u>. On bases. Every time an activity is done, the Womble gets a mark; the one with the most wins. Can be an ongoing activity throughout the camp, or a one-off activity.

12. <u>Litter Bug</u>. Each team makes a "litter bug" - a sheet of thick card (supermarket soapbox type) has a face drawn on it, and a large mouth is cut out. A dustbin bag is stuck to the back of the card, around the cutout. Then the "bug" is displayed with a sign asking people to feed the bug with its favourite food - litter.

13.   Stalking/Tracking. Wombles are very good at this. The members can try it for themselves - if they are extra quiet, they may even manage to sneak up on a real Womble (courtesy of a suitably dressed leader).

14.   Conservation. Wombles are very concerned about saving natural resources. As a starter, the members could tidy up an area of the campsite, getting it clean and tidy. As a longer term project, your group might be able to get permission to "adopt" a piece of land near to where you meet, looking after it on odd days throughout the year, planting bulbs, etc. This might get you local publicity, especially if you put up a little sign saying that your group is responsible for the new condition of the land.

GAMES

1.   Hunt the Womble. Variation 1, with different Wombles (or Womble names) on the cards.

2.   Photographing Wombles. Use the same cards as above. Each leader is given a set of one Womble, and the members have to find them and take their photographs by tagging them.

3.   Moving Burrows. Variation 2. The Wombles are moving their burrow to a new spot, and are carrying all their belongings with them. The Humans (leaders or another team) try to capture them. The side that ends with most items wins.

4.   Womble Footprints. Prepare cards with the outline of a Womble's footprint(use any foot/paw shape you like). Lay a trail for the teams, all ending at the same point, if possible, then you can see who came in first. Ensure that the next card can be seen from the location of the previous one, provided that the members look in the right place! If you use different colour felt tips to draw each team's footprints, you can cross the trails - each

team follows (or should follow!) only its own colour.

5.   Wombles and Ladders. This game is mentioned in one of the Wombles books. Prepare an obstacle/"assault" course, with some horizontal and vertical sections, perhaps using a couple of convenient trees. Send the members over it while music plays. Any member caught on a horizontal (or vertical - your choice) section when the music stops has to go back to the beginning.

6.   MacWomble's Revenge. MacWomble has gone off to sulk because the other Wombles will not let him play his bagpipes. A leader goes out with a whistle, then the members go after him. Every thirty seconds while he is standing still he has to give a blast on the whistle. As long as he keeps moving, he does not have to whistle. How long before the members can catch him?

7.   Elevenses. Wombles are very fond of eating, and Madame Cholet has to keep a sharp eye on her kitchen in case young Wombles come sneaking in for extras. Establish a base and put various items on it. Send the members out; they have to sneak up and take one of the items without being spotted. Those seen are sent back twenty steps to try again.

HOLLYWOOD

Leaders: Charlie Chaplin, Buster Keaton, Harold Lloyd, Harry Langdon, Ben Turpin, Stan Laurel, Oliver Hardy, Mack Sennett, Eric Campbell.

Teams: R.K.O., Paramount, 20th Century Fox, United Artists, Columbia, Universal, (Company logos for team logos).

ACTIVITIES

1.   Models of leader-named stars, in any format previously listed, or clay, etc.

2.   Film Set. Model or dioramas with pipe cleaner figures.

3.   Silent Films. Mimes on any subject - "give us a clue" type, miming sentences to be guessed, or miming out a given situation.

4.   Scripts. Each team writes out a script for a five minute performance, including stage directions. Scripts are swopped around between teams; after a time to read and think about it, teams act out each other's scripts. Follow with discussion - do the writers think the actors got it right? Do the actors feel that the writers were clear enough in their directions? Was there successful communication between writers and actors?

5.   "The Perils of Pauline". One team acts out a story, and stops at a high point. The next team must pick it up from there and carry on to another high point, then handing over to the third team, and so on. See where the story ends up!

6.   Stage Makeup. Let members make themselves up with play (or easily removable) makeup according to a set theme, or as they please. Maybe old man/woman, silent film villain type, etc.

7. Stage Directions. Compass. Lay out a course and give each member a list of bearings and the number of steps to take in each direction. If their compass work/paces are right, they should end up back at the start point.

8. Grauman's Chinese Theatre. This is the famous restaurant in Hollywood that has all the plaster casts of film stars outside. The members can do plaster casts of their own hand/foot.

9. Talent Show. Teams prepare items to stage at the "Hollywood Bowl". Present "Oscars" to the best performers for performing at the campfire/entertainment.

10. Lloyd at Large. Harold Lloyd was famous for his daring stunts. Present members with an obstacle/assault course.

11. "The Navigator". Map/compass.

12. Keystone Kops. Silly stunts/games.

13. Flickers. Members make cartoon "flicker pictures" which are flipped quickly to give the illusion of movement. Perhaps a leader or parent has a cine or video camera with which to make a film of the camp, or a "special item", performed by the members, that they can see when they get back home, perhaps at a special group parents' meeting.

14. "On the Road to Nowhere". Hope and Crosby "Road" films were made at Hollywood. Have a trail, go on a hike, or follow a nature trail.

15. Auditions. On bases, with general activities. Each "talent scout" marks the members' cards according to how they do at each base. This can be an ongoing activity throughout the camp - hang up the latest scoresheets so that members can see current scores.

16. Show Chaplin/Keaton/Laurel & Hardy films, <u>or</u> Disney cartoons or feature film.

17. <u>"The Trail of the Lonesome Pine"</u>. Tree spotting, bark rubbings, leaf prints.

18. <u>Right Charlies</u>. Members make "bowler hats" and canes, put on make up moustaches and see who can get the nearest to looking/walking like Chaplin.

19. <u>Custard Pie Fight</u>. Paper plates loaded with shaving foam or something similar that can be cleared up fairly easily afterwards! The custard pies can be the penalty in a game, or just a straight all-in. Be careful of people wearing glasses.

20. <u>Hollywood</u>. Members spell out "HOLLYWOOD" by finding natural objects beginning with those letters - if they can find 2 "l"s and 3 "o"s.

21. <u>Pinhole Cameras</u>. See footnote.

GAMES

1. <u>"The Great Stone Face"</u>. Buster Keaton's nickname. Two members stand a couple of feet apart and look at each other. The first to laugh (or even smile) is out, and another comes up to challenge the winner and so on.

2. <u>"The General"</u>. Variation 1, with types of steam trains, or cut out cards that assemble into a train.

3. <u>"Easy Street"</u>. Variation 2. The teams are Police, and the leaders Villains who must be arrested. Either play lives, or have each Villain bodily brought into Jail by the team, who must stay together for this!

4. <u>"Way Out West"</u>. Variation 1. Cards have sets of "brands" on them. Each team collects one brand, and

takes them, one at a time, to their base. One member of each team must stay to guard the herd, or "Rustlers" (leaders) will make off with the herd. The team with the largest suviving herd wins. Make at least three cards per member; ensure that the guard changes every now and then, to give all members a chance to go out. Any member bringing back another team's brand will be hung!

5. "The Music Box". Carrying a large (awkward rather than heavy) object over the obstacle course; relay or all in.

6. "Maiden in Distress". Any sort of "rescue" game e.g. rescue someone from the rail track (not literally!) before the train comes. Heroes vs villains! Set time limit.

7. Disney on Parade. Members parade or march around the room. When the leader shouts the name of a Disney character, everyone must mime or act it.

8. "Here's another Fine Mess!". Team captains participate in a quiz. If any fail to answer a set number of questions, their team drops them in a tub of "gunk"!

9. "Be a Charlie". Members follow a simple obstacle course but have to walk like Charlie Chaplin, balancing plastic plate or dish on head and swinging a "cane" in right hand.

10. "Disasters". A wide game where anything <u>could</u> happen (perhaps with incidents or mysteries en route for members to carry out or solve), and frequently <u>does</u>.

11. "Capitol Records". This recording company started in Hollywood, signing up many of the movie stars. Play a singing game e.g. choose a subject - each team takes turns to sing the opening bars of a song on that subject. Teams drop out or lose a life when they fail to come up with a song.

PINHOLE CAMERAS

Kodak Limited have an information sheet on making and using pinhole cameras.

Write to: Kodak Limited
                         PO Box 66
                         Hemel Hempstead
                         Herts HP1 1JU
                         Tel: (0442) 61122

and enclose an SAE.

PIRATES

Leaders: Long John Silver, Blackbeard, Anne Bonney, Mary Read, Captain Flint, Captain Teach, Ben Gunn, Henry Morgan

Teams: Corsairs, Privateers, Buccaneers, Brigands

ACTIVITIES

1. Models. Pirate costumes.

2. Pirate Ship. Each team makes a pirate ship from paper/card/odds and ends.

3. Diorama. For either of the above.

4. Handicraft. Members make pirate hats (front panel with a band to go round the back of the head; older members could try "proper" hats), card eyepatches and cutlasses.

5. Yo Ho Ho. Each team prepares an item for the camp-fire/entertainment - perhaps a pirate song or sketch.

6. Long John Silver. Members make a crutch out of natural objects, finding a suitably shaped and sized piece of wood and adapting it. This item can lead into a discussion on disabilities if desired.

7. Treasure Island. Give members/teams a map of the campsite, with features left in but all names removed. They have to name the maps in Pirate style.

8. Treasure Maps. As an extension to the above, give teams absolutely blank maps, with only the campsite boundary and the north point marked in. They have to map the area, producing a map drawn to a set scale.

9.   <u>Money bags</u>. On bases. Each member has/makes a small cloth bag and goes round to various bases. For every activity they complete, they get a "gold piece" to put into their money bags. The bases can be on any theme or non theme activities.

10.   <u>Parrots</u>. Members make a paper/card parrot, either to fix onto their shoulders, or to sit on a card ring which can be hung up. 3-D parrots could be made from odds and ends, or cut from material, stuffed, and decorated.

11.   <u>Press Gang</u>. Teams produce a camp newspaper, either in teams or all in, with articles, drawings, and so on.

12.   <u>Digging for Treasure</u>. Tidying up an area of the camp-site - perhaps digging the Warden's garden for him?

13.   <u>Mastmaking</u>. Each team makes a flagpole out of bamboo or cane or heavier spars, depending on their age and ability. There should be a piece to tie off the halyards. The flagpole could be a simple upright design, or as any design that the teams feel they can build successfully.

14.   <u>Flags.</u> Teams make flags and fly them from their flag-poles. This can lead in to your organisation's flag if it has one, the Union Flag, and others.

15.   <u>Pirate Cabins</u>. Shelters.

16. <u>Candle Lanterns</u>. Members make a square lantern with a card frame and clear plastic/clingfilm windows, perhaps with a nightlight inside (in which case, have them put a double base, with a hole in the upper one to hold the nightlight still, and air vents in the lantern - one side must be able to open to enable them to get inside it). If candles are used, stress fire precautions.

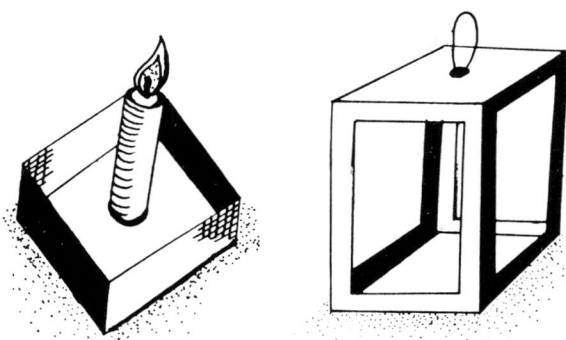

17. <u>Pirate Boats</u>. Matchbox boats, perhaps with tiny flags at the "masthead".

18. <u>Treasure Trail</u>. Tracking.

19. <u>Stories</u>. Read the members pirate stories, and let them illustrate them with mimes, plays, pictures, etc.

20. <u>Exploring Treasure Island</u>. Nature trail, tree spotting,leaf/bark prints.

21. <u>Pirate Messages</u>. Morse, Semaphore, or International Flag signalling.

22. <u>Shipwrecked</u>. The pirates have been marooned on a desert island; they have to survive until a rescue ship arrives. Backwoods cooking, fires, bivouacs; any other "survival" type activity, to whatever degree the members' abilities make practical.

GAMES

1. ...And a bottle of rum. Variation 1, with the cards carrying pictures of bottles of grog which the teams collect.

2. Pirates' Earrings. Loops of yellow/orange wool as a tracking trail, or as a variation 1.

3. Rig ship for action. Knotting relay.

4. Mutiny on the Bunty. (Not a misprint!). Members are mutineers who have taken over the ship. Leaders are the Officers who must capture/arrest them.

5. Walking the Plant. Either a silly stunts session or an "assault" course, perhaps tree climbing.

6. Navel Action. As "Sailors", game 6.

7. Shipwreck. Variation 1. Cards carry pictures/names of pieces of equipment which the shipwrecked pirates must collect to survive on their desert island.

Some games and activities can be borrowed from "Sailors" and slightly adapted to fit the Pirate theme.

WILD WEST

Leaders: Wyatt Earp, Morgan Earp, Virgil Earp, Doc Holliday, Annie Oakley, Butch Cassidy, Sam Bass, Pat McGarrett, The Man with No Name (Warden).

Teams: Rustlers, Outlaws, Posse.

Places:

Leaders' tents	Sherriff's office
Members' tents	Corral
Dining area	Chuck Wagon
Local shops	Saloon/general store
First aid area	Boot Hill
Kitchen/stores	Ranch house
Campsite	Deadwood City

ACTIVITIES

1.   <u>Models</u>. Cowboy costumes.

2.   <u>Stagecoach & horses</u>. Models, either cut out and stick, odds and ends, or flat drawings.

3.   <u>Deadwood City</u>. Model cowboy town, with card buildings and pipe cleaner figures.

4.   <u>Diorama</u>. For any of the above.

5.   <u>Guns</u>. Members make six shooters, either from odds and ends, or out of natural objects. They then make gunbelts from material and holsters from card.

6.   <u>Hats</u>. Members make cowboy hats and spurs from card.

7.   <u>Chaps</u>. Members make chaps (leggings) and waistcoats from strong paper (if you use brown paper, the members might be accused of rustling!).

8.   <u>Fires</u>.

9.   <u>Cooking</u>. Bangers/bacon and beans, cooked over their own fires.

10.   <u>Stories</u>. Read Wild West stories, true or fictional, and let the members illustrate with plays, pictures, etc.

11.   <u>Telegraph</u>. Long distance communication: string telephone, Morse, Semaphore.

12.   <u>Tracking</u>.

13.   <u>Smoke Signals</u>. As "Indians", activity 18.

14.   <u>Branding</u>. Pieces of wood or leather can be branded with an organisation's badge. Fix a badge securely to the end of a stretched out wire coat hanger; pad the end or provide a hand grip, and heat the badge in a fire, then press the "branding iron" onto a piece of wood. Only the brand and a short length of wire should be over the fire; embers heat better than roaring flames. The members could make sun brands with magnifying glass/burning glass. Focus the light down to as small and tight a beam as possible; after a while the wood will blacken. Move the glass slowly, and members can burn their names into the wood, personalising the (leader made) fire brands. Very young members can make "brands" by potato printing, etc.

15. Lassoing. Each member has a length of rope, with a loop made (the "proper" way of fixing the loop is with a "Honda" knot). They then practice lassoing objects from a distance which increases as they get better. This can lead into throwing a rope for rescue - how to coil and throw a rope properly without it tangling.

16. Rope Spinning. Cowboys could do stunts with their lariats, spinning and making patterns with the loop. See if the members can do it, too.

17. Fires can be started with a lens; see if the members can get a fire going without any matches at all. (The sun is rather a vital ingredient for this to succeed!).

18. Water Divining. The West is a very dry country, and water is much sought after. Try dowsing, either with traditional hazel twigs, or as in the sketch.

19. Cowboy Skills. Knots and lashings for cowboys' work - highwayman's hitch for tying their horses, lashings for fixing fences, etc.

20. Gold Rush. On bases. Members do activities, and get "gold nuggets" for every one they complete successfully.

21. Riding. Visit a riding school/stable.

22. Observation. Lay out cards with different symbols/"brands". The members look for one minute, then close their eyes. Remove one of the cards, and the members have to say which card is missing. Or, give teams a set of brand cards, and they have to reconstruct the sequence in which the original cards were laid.

23. Teams prepare an item/song for the campfire/entertainment.

24. Sunday go to meetin'. Teams prepare a section of the main act of worship.

25. Deadwood Stage. Teams build a moveable stagecoach, out of boxes, odds and ends, or natural materials. Perhaps all the teams can get together to build a life-size(ish) stagecoach.

26. Deadwood. Tree spotting, perhaps the burning qualities of different kinds of wood; making/whittling objects out of dead wood, camp gadgets, etc.

27. Prairie Schooners. Teams make "covered wagons".

28. Deadwood Daily. Camp newspaper. Perhaps the members could "print" their editions with the aid of a small printing set, typesetting and printing their own sections of the day's(?) edition.

GAMES

1. Horseshoe tossing. Members make horseshoes out of strong card, and have a contest to see who can get theirs the closest to an upright pole - ideally, the horseshoes should end up around the pole. Or perhaps you can acquire real horseshoes.

2. Sharpshooting. Members armed with a squeezy bottle have to shoot down paper plates tossed into the air.

3. Gunfight at the OK Corral. All in squeezy bottle/water pistol fight, perhaps with team vs team, ambushing and firing on others; or members vs leaders.

4. Round up. As game 4, "Hollywood".

5. Tracking rustlers. Tracking trail, perhaps with "horse-shoe" prints for each team to follow: the trail can split up as the Rustlers separate; the trails can cross and re-cross, if each team's cards are colour coded.

6. Pony Express. Variation 2, with the Outlaws trying to stop the Pony Express riders from getting through with the mail.

7. Rodeo. Silly stunts/games on the cowboy theme: "bucking bronco", etc.

8. Stampede! One member is "it", and has to round up the other members by hitting them below the knee with a soft ball. Once hit, they join the first member. Last one caught wins.

9. Cactus Flower. The teams have to cross the desert, navigating from cactus to cactus until they reach the other side. Trail, or compass bearings from point to point, with the next bearing written on the "cactus" at the end of each stage.

10. The "hoot owl" trail. The outlaws are planning to raid the ranch house. All members are taken by a leader a distance away from the camp and sent off (the leader blows a whistle to let the "ranch hands" back at base know that the game has started). The outlaws have to sneak past the defenders and get to the ranch. An optional dark game.

SPACE

Leaders: Orion, Andromeda, Sirius, Aquila, Perseus, Antares, Hercules, Cygnus, etc.

Teams: a) Mercury, Gemini, Apollo, Vostok, Soyuz, Columbia, etc.
b) Vega, Mars, Jupiter, Polaris, Saturn, Alpha Centauri, etc.

Places:
Leaders' tents	Mission Control
Members' tents	Asteroid Belt
Dining area	L(a)unch Pad
Washrooms	Splashdown
Campsite	Cape Kennedy

ACTIVITIES

1.   Models. Each member costumes an astronaut (supply plenty of tinfoil), and adds backpacks, and equipment for the astronaut.

2.   Space ships. Each team constructs a space ship from card/odds and ends: perhaps an existing type of craft, or a futuristic one.

3.   B.E.M.. Each member designs and builds a "Bug Eyed Monster" in any handicraft format. Once built, they have to say where it lives, and what it eats: this must agree with its appearance - an alien with great big fangs is not likely to be a vegetarian (though it might be a Vegan).

4.   Diorama. For any/all of the above. Perhaps all three can be combined in one diorama, with the astronaut meeting the alien beside his ship - the landscape would be suitably "out of this world".

5. <u>Zap guns</u>. Members design and build model zap guns, as weird and wonderful as they like, in any handicraft format. Once they have been made, perhaps inventors can explain how their zap gun works!

6. <u>Mural</u>. Each member makes a panel with a space theme - perhaps a super space city, or a "wraparound" alien landscape scene.

7. <u>Helmets</u>. Members make space helmets from card/paper. NOTE: if they decide to make "goldfish bowl" type helmets, make sure they realise the importance of having air holes in it! Perhaps the visors of such helmets can be taken as read - leave the face uncovered.

8. <u>Stories</u>. Read stories - either real space-travel, or stories of the constellations, from the Greek legends, or "space pirate" fiction. Members can then illustrate with pictures, plays, etc.

9. <u>Indoor Astronomy</u>. With card tubes covered at one end with a piece of black paper, with has pinpricks in the shape of the constellations, to let the light through when held up to the light. Brighter stars get bigger holes. Start with the basic, easily recognised ones: Great Bear, Orion, Casseiopeia, and work to others: Taurus, Leo, Andromeda. Or include some Southern Hemisphere constellation, which the members may never get to see for themselves, to teach them that the sky does not look the same all the way round the earth.

10. <u>Skylab</u>. Teams design a space station, inside and out, and build the outside, with docking bays, and so on. If you have a hut, these can be hung up on display.

11. Rockets. Sellotape a straw to a straw-section. Attach the neck of a balloon to one end of the straw, and thread a length of cord through the section. Attach the cord across a distance, keeping it taut. Hold the straw, and blow into it to partly inflate the balloon. When it is released, the straw will shoot along the string as the escaping air pushes the straw forward. This could be made into a game: which team's rocket will reach the Space Station first?

12. Signalling to Mars. "Marse" Code.

13. Navigation. With the stars, and compass.

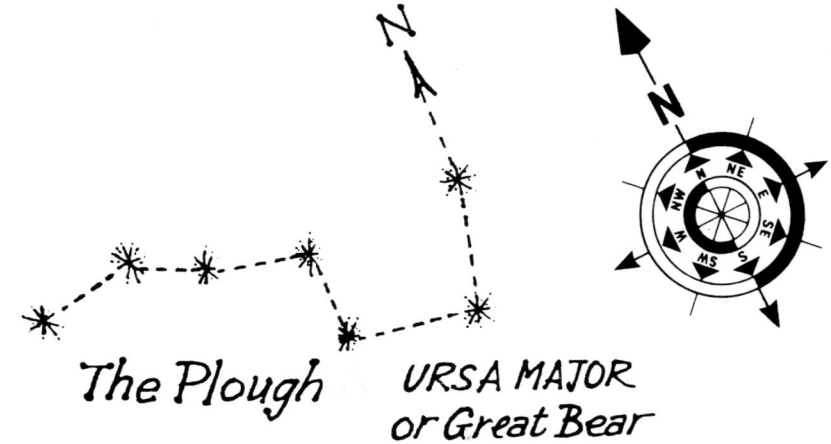

The Plough   URSA MAJOR
or Great Bear

14. Planet Earth. Supply teams with blank maps of the world. Can they fill in the countries (or even the correct boundaries of their own country)? This leads into International items - One World, One People, and anything else you want to bring in.

15. Diplomatic Mission. A party of delegates has arrived from a distant planet to trade with Earth. Unfortunately, they cannot speak English, and members cannot speak their language. They have to devise a method of sign language, of communicating without a spoken language.

16. <u>Captain's Log</u>. Members keep a camp diary, either individually, or in teams, or all contributing to one main diary. If the latter two, try to ensure that all members contribute something. If individual, collect them at the end of camp and write them out into an exercise/scrapbook, using their exact words, to use as a display item on future occasions.

17. <u>Woomeras</u>. The Australian rocket base at Woomera was named after an Aboriginal spear thrower. Members could make their own woomeras. A tube of thick card (dress material centre) is cut in half to make two semi circular channels. A piece of card is fitted across one end, with a small twig sticking out a bit inside the tube to make a stop to hold the spear. Two thongs are fitted to the front end, long enough so that the member can hold them while also holding the tube at the point of balance. The "spear" may be a smaller tube, or a garden cane. Its end is notched to fit into the stop. The member swings back, and throws overarm, straight armed, letting go of the woomera while holding the thongs. The back end of the woomera rises with the momentum, and the spear is slung much harder and further than could be achieved by hand alone. Because the back end rises, the effect is as if the member had a six foot arm - the lever principle applies. If woomeras are made, a clearly defined time and place should be laid down for using them - they are NOT toys to be used against random objects or other people.

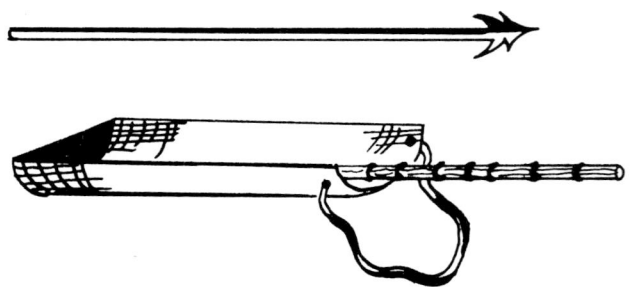

18. Rocket Launcher. A car foot pump and a supply of washing up liquid bottles are needed for this. Remove the caps from the bottles; one is held down over the nozzle of the pump (person holding the bottle must keep their face back). The bottle is pumped full of air - the person will feel the bottle fighting to take off - when it is released, it will shoot up into the air. See who can get their rocket the highest.

19. Astronaut Training. Keep fit, exercises, etc.

20. Robots. Teams make a robot from cartons, odds and ends, etc. Moving parts add extra points! Could be run on bases, with each activity completed giving teams another part of the robot - either on paper, or a real part, so that they can have a fully assembled robot by the end of camp.

21. Computer Talk. Computers need very precise instructions to do the job properly. If they are not told exactly what to do, they do not do it. See if members can express themselves clearly and exactly - do they really mean it when they tell someone to hang on for a minute, or go jump in a lake? Perhaps you could have a session in which everybody does exactly what they are told, and see the confusion that results!

22. GTV (Galactic Television). Teams prepare an item for the campfire/entertainment. Perhaps teams could devise a "Wish you were here" type holiday programme for package tours to other planets.

23. Act of Worship. Teams contribute sections, perhaps on the theme of One World, prayers for astronauts, etc.

GAMES

MARTIAN INVASION (Can be run on consecutive days over the camp).

Phase 1

The Martians have invaded earth, and all the people are on the run. Variation 2: the members go out, and the Martians (leaders) give them a start before pursuing them; see how many Earthlings can be captured in a given time.

Phase 2

The Earthlings are gathered into small groups (teams) and must all get together at their main base, which they can then fortify against the Martians. Unfortunately, Martians are patrolling the area, with zap guns (squeezy bottles filled with water). The Earthlings have no weapons, so they must try to sneal past the Martians without getting zapped.

Phase 3

Now the Earthlings have reached their base, and have fortified it. They have armed themselves with zap guns, and a supply of ammunition (buckets of water). Now they must repel the Martians, who are trying to get into the base to capture the Earthlings' flag. Can the Earthlings stop them? (all in water fight).

Phase 4

The Earthlings have invented a machine that will destroy the Martians. It is too big to be carried in one piece, so groups of Earthlings have to carry it in sections past the Martians, getting it to their Command base. The teams have lives, or small objects which must be got from one base to the other. The side that ends up with the most pieces at the end of time wins.

Phase 5

Supply drop. The Earthlings have been dropped supplies to help them fight the Martians. Unfortunately, the drop fell wide, and the supplies are scattered all around the area. Teams have to find all of their supplies (cards) and take them back to base without getting zapped by a Martian.

Phase 6

The Martians are on the run, the Earthlings are winning the battle. There are a few surviving Martians in the area, which the Earthlings must zap. Teams must go out together for this, since the Martians have to be hit by a number of zap guns to kill them. How long before all the Martians are zapped?

2.   Astronauts. Space Olympics; silly stunts and games.

3.   Space ship on the rocks. As the standard game, but with space age key words.

4.   Space battleships. As Battleships (Sailors, game 16) with rocket ships, starships, etc.

5.   Shooting stars. Any sort of target game.